The Good Shepherd

John 10:1–18 for children

Written by Joanne Bader • Illustrated by Larry Nolte

Arch® Books
Copyright © 1999 Concordia Publishing House
3558 S. Jefferson Avenue, St. Louis, MO 63118-3968
Manufactured in Colombia

Our dear Lord told this story once
To people that He knew.
A story 'bout a flock of sheep
And of their shepherd too.

"The shepherd knows his sheep," He said.
"He knows each one by name.
They are his own. He watches them
And loves them all the same.

"They know his voice. He calls to them.
They follow where he leads.
They trust that he will care for them,
Provide for all their needs.

"If thieves and robbers creep around
Or climb into the pen,
The sheep refuse to go with them.
They know that they're mean men.

"Sometimes a sheep will stray away
From others in the bunch.
The shepherd goes and looks for him
And brings him back 'fore lunch.

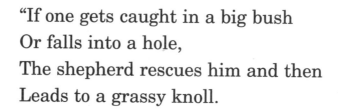

"If one gets caught in a big bush
Or falls into a hole,
The shepherd rescues him and then
Leads to a grassy knoll.

"Suppose a wolf attacks the flock
And scatters them about?
The shepherd would not run away,
He'd chase the wolf right out!

"He leads the sheep back to the fold,
Each ram and every ewe.
He'd give his life to save his sheep
If that's what he must do."

What does this story mean to us,
The children of today?
Could we be like those sheep and lambs
When we go out to play?

JESUS LOVES THE SHE

The heavenly Father sent His Son
To be our Shepherd dear.
We are the sheep He loves so much.
He always wants us near.

JESUS IS THE GOOD SHEPHERD

He knows each one of us by name.
Now listen for His voice,
And when He calls just follow Him.
Be happy and rejoice.

When Satan, who's the evil one,
Would steal us all away,
Jesus, our Shepherd kind and true,
Gives us the strength to stay.

He blesses us and cares for us.
He stays right by our side.
He's our protector, bold and brave,
Our leader and our guide.

He gave His life for all our sins
And rose on Easter morn.
He is the gate to heaven above.
We'll enter there newborn.

Jesus, my Shepherd, hold me close
And lead me day by day.
Please let me always hear Your voice
And follow it, I pray.

Dear Parents:

Children learn best when they see, smell, hear, taste, and touch things. This is called concrete learning. When something makes sense in their world it becomes a part of learning for children. Yet, we often ask them to understand abstract concepts without helping these concepts make sense in their world.

This book will help your child relate to the concept of Jesus as the Good Shepherd through descriptions of His love and care for us in real, concrete images. Take time to talk with your child about the many ways that Jesus cares for us as a shepherd would protect his sheep.

Make a family picture of sheep. Turn your hands upside down with your thumbs pointing out straight. Trace around each hand making the thumb the head of the sheep and the four fingers the feet. Add cotton balls for fluff and other features. Add a picture of Jesus to help you remember that He loves you as a Shepherd loves His sheep.

The Editor